STARKIDS
IN AMERICA

LAND of the FREE because of the BRAVE.

THE CONSTITUTION of the UNITED STATES, WAS BORN HERE— SEPTEMBER, 1787

By Britt Crennell

Do something today that makes you proud!
—The StarKids

I would like to thank the members of the Religious Society of Friends (Quakers) in Pennsylvania for making information about the Quakers accessible to others at the Arch Street Meeting House and those at the meetinghouse itself for taking the time to review the applicable chapter and confirm that the information is correct.

I am also grateful to the Friends Historical Library of Swarthmore for providing an illustration of Benjamin Lay.

StarKids is an educational work of fiction which includes information about real places, historical figures, and events. However, the characters and incidents in the story are a product of the author's imagination. Any character resemblance to an actual person is coincidental.

The settings and location, although real, are used in a fictitious manner.

Civics4Kids
Davis, CA
StarKids.in.America@gmail.com
ISBN 979-8-9869858-5-5

Here's what students say about *StarKids in America: Pennsylvania*

Another amazing book about the StarKids and their adventures. I love these awesome stories that are jam-packed with things to learn. I wish all my schoolbooks were written like this. Keep going!
—**Kavi R.**, The Kid Consultant, 5th grade

It's a fantastic book, one of the best books I've ever read. The humor is hilarious. I learned quite a bit and would definitely recommend the book to my friends.
—**Ciara M.**, 4th grade

I love this book. It's very good, and funny too. So are the illustrations. I learned about American History, how the American flag was designed and that the bald eagle is our national bird. Love this book!
—**Ismael R.**, 4th grade

StarKids is a very funny book. It kept me laughing and guessing until the end. My favorite character is Lucy, a goofy and funny bald eagle.
—**Calvin C.**, 4th grade

I thought the book was really funny. It was a fun way to learn about the the First Amendment.
—**Kendall C.**, 4th grade

I love the book. The jokes are funny. I didn't even know about the U.S. Constitution before I read it. Now I do!
—**Zoey M.**, 4th grade

THE CAST AND THEIR FAVES

ANGIE
HOBBY: I like skateboard competitions (and I love to win).
SUBJECT: Robotics
SAYING: I'm down!

PIPER
HOBBY: You can find me in the science lab doing cool experiments.
SUBJECT: Science
SAYING: I know, right?

ZANE
HOBBY: I'm always up for BMX and LAX (lacrosse).
SUBJECT: American History
SAYING: Let's go!

DIRK
HOBBY: I'm a singer, songwriter and guitarist.
SUBJECT: English (I like creative writing and poetry).
SAYING: Let's get this party started!

LUCY
HOBBY: Dressing in fancy clothes.
SUBJECT: Theater (Some people call me a drama queen).
SAYING: Don't be a bird brain.

GEORGE
HOBBY: Scouting for prey
SUBJECT: Civics (As a citizen, I know my rights and duties).
SAYING: Mind your own birdswax.

MAC
HOBBY: Hanging out at dog parks
SUBJECT: How to sniff out bones
SAYING: Bone Apetit

The book series *StarKids in America* is aligned to Common Core State Standards for Language Arts (4th–5th grade). Each book has a companion workbook that follows it, chapter by chapter.

QUIET PLEASE!
FUN LEARNING IN PROGRESS!

VOCABULARY

Each chapter includes 10 vocabulary words, all of which are underlined. The definition of each word is in the Glossary at the back of the book.

PROLOGUE

THE STARS HAVE VANISHED FROM THE AMERICAN FLAG. NO ONE CAN FIGURE OUT WHY. CAN YOU?

One day, Dirk's mom brought home a bucket with an old, musty flag inside. That afternoon, Dirk was playing his guitar when he lost his balance and fell into the bucket on top of the flag. All of a sudden he was in a city park staring up at Lucy, a wacky bald eagle, perched in a tree. She told him that the *magic* flag—the flag in the bucket—had transported him to Philadelphia, the very place the U.S. Constitution was written.

Lucy's supposed to help whoever has the flag solve the mystery of the missing stars and restore them to the flag. But she wasn't sure kids could do it. Luckily, Dirk convinced her to give him and his friends—Angie, Zane, and Piper—a chance.

To crack the case, they'd have to *flagtag:* tag the flag and instantly be transported to places where they can find clues. So, Dirk, Piper, and Angie *flagtagged* to different places in Delaware and learned important facts about the state. When they got home, they figured out that the first clue was the word *perseverance* which means to keep trying even when things get tough.

Presto!

Like magic, a single star appeared on the magic flag. Can you believe it? Finding the first clue earned a star! Now, it's time for the StarKids to *flagtag* to Pennsylvania to search for the second clue.

Come join the quest to save the American flag.

To help us find the second clue, you need to know some American history. A long time ago, there were 13 British colonies in North America.

Many colonists (Patriots) were unhappy because they felt the king of England treated them unfairly.

The Patriots decided to break away from England and create their own country.

But the British wanted to keep control of the colonies, so the Patriots had to fight for independence.

The war was called the American Revolutionary War.

The Patriots won the war. The 13 British colonies became the first American states, and the United States of America was born.

CHAPTER
One

DIRK'S A NO-SHOW

Who would've guessed that Dirk would mess things up?

It's time for the StarKids to go to Pennsylvania to search for the clue. Piper, Zane, and Angie made it to the school flag but Dirk didn't show up. He gave his backpack to Angie when the final bell rang and told her that he'd see her in a few minutes. That was 20 minutes ago. No one has seen him since.

Zane rubs his chin like he's a spy trying to solve a top-secret case. "Do you think he forgot?"

"No way," replies Piper. "The magic flag's in his backpack. He wouldn't just give it to Angie and ditch us."

"If we don't leave now," says Zane, "we'll get back too late."

Angie gives him a dirty look. "We're not going without him. If he doesn't get here, we'll go tomorrow."

Zane shoves his hands in his pockets. "We need some rules for a time like this. Should we leave if he's a no-show?"

Angie sets Dirk's backpack next to the flagpole. "We're a team! We're solving this mystery together."

"But we don't have much time," Zane reminds her. "If we don't find thirteen clues fast, the flag will fade. Forever!"

Piper takes a red notebook out of her backpack.

"You're right," she says. "We need rules. I'll write them down."

"We should vote on them too," says Zane. "We'll be a <u>democracy</u>. We each get equal say."

Boing! A big rubber ball smacks Angie in the head.

Angie whirls around to a bunch of wide-eyed kids. "Who threw that?" she yells. "Fess up!"

No one <u>utters</u> a sound, except Billy who's laughing his head off.

"Sorry Angie," he howls. "We're playing dodgeball. And your head got in the way."

Angie looks at Billy for a split second, then takes off after him. "You threw it on purpose!"

"Duh!" Billy runs in the opposite direction

3

<u>flailing</u> his arms and laughing so everyone knows he's not scared.

"We'll never get to Pennsylvania," says Piper. "Dirk ditched us, and now, Angie's…uh…distracted."

There's a burst of cheers as Angie and Billy race across the blacktop. She's the fastest runner in fourth grade. Billy, not so much.

"Bully!" Angie screams. "Scaredy cat!"

Grant is at the bike rack watching as they run toward him. My bike, he thinks. I'll give her my bike. While he's taking off the lock, Billy gets there, grabs his own bike and rides out onto the soccer field.

When Angie gets there, Grant holds out his bike. "Here! Take this!"

"Thanks, Grant!" she says, panting. "But don't give me flowers anymore. That was just weird."

Angie hops on the bike and rides as fast as she can onto the soccer field. She can feel her legs burning as she pedals faster and faster.

"I'm right behind you, Bully!" she yells. "Scumbag!"

Billy wonders what Angie plans to do if she catches up to him. Fight? Rap battle? Glare?

Maybe I should stop and find out, he thinks. This oughta be fun.

He squeezes the brakes and slows down. As Angie closes in on him, Billy starts looking big. Really big. Gigantic! And she starts to worry. Why's he stopping? What should I do now? Maybe this chase wasn't a good idea.

She skids to a stop and jumps off the bike.

Billy lets out a fake laugh. "Looking at your face reminds me that I forgot to put out the garbage."

Angie's <u>stumped</u>; not sure what to say. She didn't think this through, *all* the way through. Billy's the biggest kid in school. Three times her size. Now what?

Billy leans over his handlebars. "Are you gonna beat me up?"

Angie puts on her meanest face. Billy isn't <u>fazed</u>. He's playing it cool. Billy, the cool bully.

"You threw that ball at me on purpose," she says.

Billy hops off his bike and flips down the kickstand. "Yeah. So what?"

"Well…uh…," Angie stammers. "Well…uh… you're a total jerk."

Billy smiles so wide Angie can see peanut butter on his teeth. "Thank you!"

Angie tries to think of a clever <u>insult</u>, a real zinger. But her mind is blank. Not that it would

make any difference. Billy's proud to be a jerk…a *total* jerk.

Meanwhile, Zane, Piper and the other Cub Club kids are standing on the edge of the blacktop watching the <u>showdown</u>.

"We need to get her back here," Piper tells Zane. "We gotta do something."

Zane spots a bull horn outside a portable classroom, dashes over and grabs it. "Let's cheer!"

Piper gives him a strange look. "Huh? Cheer?"

Zane raises the bullhorn to his mouth, and hollers:

"Hey! Hey! Billy!
Don't you feel silly?
You might rule the school.
But she caught you, fool."

The kids on the playground erupt in laughter.

Zane chuckles to himself. Didn't make much sense, he thinks. But it rhymed. I'll try another one.

He waves his free hand and starts up again:

"Billy! You got blown away.
Angie beat your butt today."

The kids clap, and join in:

"Billy! You got blown away.
Angie beat your butt today."

Angie eyes Billy who's watching the kids clap and cheer. His big sneer slowly fades, and his face turns so red she almost feels sorry for him.

Almost.

"How do you feel about being a *total jerk* now?" she asks.

Billy doesn't answer. Just stares. Angie's never seen him this quiet.

She picks up the bike, acting all calm and cool. "Maybe next time, you'll think twice before you throw a ball at my head."

As she pedals away, she can feel his eyes burning into her back. Weirdly, she also feels a <u>sense</u> of <u>accomplishment</u> like she beat an <u>undefeated</u> competitor in a skateboard event.

And it feels good!

CHILLIN' WITH THE PRINCI-PAL

If I don't get outta here fast, thinks Dirk, the clue journey is <u>doomed</u>.

He's sitting with the school principal, Mr. Waddick, trying not to look at the <u>tuft</u> of black hair on top of his head. It looks like an ocean wave. Dirk thinks if Mr. Waddick dyed the *wave* purple and picked up an electric guitar, he'd look like a punk rocker. But he doesn't look so punky now, glaring across his desk at Dirk.

Dirk's on edge, glancing around like he's never seen the principal's office before. He has though. Plenty of times. He likes to think of *office visits* as part of the elementary school experience, but today he's stressed out, <u>fidgeting</u> with papers and tapping his feet like crazy. If the StarKids don't make it to Pennsylvania, it's his fault. The librarian, Ms. Livre, sent him to the office for using the copy machine without permission.

From the open window behind Mr. Waddick, they can hear the schoolyard noise. Dirk needs to get out there. Fast!

"My friends are waiting for me," he says. "Can I go tell them I'll be late?"

Mr. Waddick takes a red apple out of his drawer. It's so shiny, it looks like someone waxed it. "What time are you supposed to meet them?"

"Three o'clock."

Mr. Waddick glances at his watch. "It's 3:20. They know you're late."

Dirk <u>slouches</u> in the chair. Things aren't looking good.

Principal Waddick bites his apple, and asks, "Do you know why you're here?"

"Yeah." Dirk holds up the papers. "I didn't ask permission to use the copy machine. Uh…can I do my detention at lunch? I'm sorta busy after school these days."

Mr. Waddick puts down the apple and <u>motions</u> for the papers. Dirk hands them to him and sits quietly while Mr. Waddick reads them over. Dirk copied pages from a book about the Constitution of the United States. Since the Constitution was written and adopted in Pennsylvania, he thinks it might have something to do with the clue.

Mr. Waddick raises his eyebrows. "Hmm…the U.S. Constitution," he says, curiously. "Are you doing a report on it?"

"Nope," replies Dirk. "Just doing some research. It's a famous <u>historic</u> <u>document</u> that I'm learning about."

Mr. Waddick smiles for the first time. "That's great! What have you learned?"

Dirk doesn't hesitate. "Well, when the United States became a country, the leaders wrote rules for how everything should run."

"Those rules are called the Articles of Confederation," adds Mr. Waddick. "The Articles were the first constitution."

"Uh-huh," says Dirk. "But the Articles didn't help much. The first thirteen states acted like separate countries. Not one country. So, the leaders got together to change the Articles…and ended up writing a whole new constitution."

Mr. Waddick smiles, <u>impressed</u>. "You're right," he says. "The country was in shambles because there wasn't a strong central government. The U.S. Constitution created a stronger federal government and a new plan for how the federal and state governments should operate." He leans back in his big leather chair and puts his hands behind his head. "Did you know that the Constitution also protects your special rights."

Dirk moves to the edge of his seat, all ears. "I have *special* rights?"

If he could pick his *special* rights, he'd have the right to eat pizza all day. Play VR video games all night. And make every day a holiday.

FIRST AMENDMENT: RAPPS

R—RELIGION   Freedom of RELIGION

A—ASSEMBLY   Freedom of ASSEMBLY

P—PRESS   Freedom of PRESS

P—PETITION   Right to PETITION

S—SPEECH   Freedom of SPEECH

Rockin' with the U.S. Constitution.

Mr. Waddick laughs out loud. "Dirk, not just you. All people in America have special rights. The Constitution protects our freedoms…like the right to practice any religion, share our opinions, and even protest peacefully to show the government how we feel about certain issues."

Dirk thinks this over. "Those rights don't seem all that *special.*"

Mr. Waddick frowns at him. "Before our Founding Fathers wrote the Constitution, there were few guarantees of freedom. People worried that the government would take their freedoms away."

Dirk has plenty of questions, but no time.

"Uh…can I have the copies back?" he asks. "I gotta go."

Principal Waddick hands him the papers. "Dirk, there's something we need to discuss. Did you tell Ms. Livre you planned to visit Pennsylvania today?"

Dirk nods. "Yeah, I did."

When Ms. Livre asked him why he made the copies, Dirk told her the truth; he was going to Pennsylvania after school. Bad idea! She thought he was trying to be funny.

Mr. Waddick picks up the shiny apple and chomps on it. "You need to learn when it's okay to joke and when it's not. Do you understand?"

Dirk nods again. He's starting to feel like a bobble head.

There's a sudden uproar outside; kids yelling and screaming. Mr. Waddick swivels his chair to see out the window and Dirk stands up to look. Angie's chasing Billy across the blacktop.

Dirk notices that she doesn't have his backpack and wonders what she did with it. The magic flag's inside!

Mr. Waddick closes the window. "I'm happy that you're learning about the Constitution, but if you violate school rules again, I'll have to give you detentions."

Dirk's eyes go wide. "*Detentions?* More than one?"

I've already botched up one clue journey, he thinks. If I get detentions, the team will have to go without me.

Or else the stars and stripes will be lost forever.

BEING SUPER FANTASTIC AT BAD IDEAS

It's too late to go to Pennsylvania, and Dirk is bummed out, *big time.* He knows it's his fault.

Secretary Smith is on the telephone when he and Mr. Waddick step out of his office. She has silver hair with big curls that look frozen in place. Dirk wonders if she sprays her hair with super glue in the morning, so it stays stuck all day.

"I know Junior is a smart boy," she says into the phone. "But we can't have him flushing frogs down our toilets."

Mr. Waddick sets a hand on Dirk's shoulder. "How's school going?"

Dirk knows when Mr. Waddick asks about school, he's really asking about his grades.

"Great! I have all Bs," he tells him. "I'm good with that! The guy who <u>designed</u> the American flag did it for a school project and his teacher gave him a B-."

17

Mr. Waddick <u>furrows</u> his eyebrows. "Robert Heft? The man who designed the 50-star flag?"

Dirk smiles brightly. "That's him! He got a B-for the <u>design</u>. Congress had a contest for the best flag design. He entered the contest and won! So, I'm happy with all Bs."

Principal Waddick has a <u>gleam</u> in his eye. "You should be."

Secretary Smith raises her voice, still on the phone. "I know frogs can swim. But we don't want them swimming in our toilets."

Dirk <u>gestures</u> at a large poster of a bald eagle with an American flag in the background.

"Did you know that Ben Franklin didn't  think the bald eagle should be our national bird?" he asks. "He called it a mean coward because it bullies and steals food from other birds. He said that turkeys have more courage."

"What about you?" asks Mr. Waddick. "Do you think the turkey would make a good national bird?"

Dirk imagines a turkey on the poster. "Not really."

"For me, a turkey doesn't fit the part," says Mr. Waddick. "But eagles look <u>majestic</u> and <u>sophisticated</u>."

Dirk imagines Lucy. Majestic? Sophisti- cated? Not quite.

"Most bald eagles look pretty cool," he laughs, "as long as they're not wearing weird clothes or a wig."

Mr. Waddick lets out a <u>hearty</u> chuckle. "You and your sense of

humor." He sets a hand on Dirk's shoulder. "Before you leave, I must ask. Do you still plan to go to Pennsylvania today?"

"Nope, too late for that."

"Alright, get to Cub Club, but remember, there's a right and wrong time to joke."

Dirk promises Mr. Waddick that it won't happen again, waves to Secretary Smith and leaves the office. She doesn't see him, too busy talking.

Dirk jogs down the hall past the classrooms

and bursts out the exit. He sees Zane and Piper at the portable classroom putting the bullhorn back and breaks into a sprint.

When he reaches them, he's short of breath.

"Sorry," he gasps. "Ms. Livre sent me to the office for making copies."

Zane gives him a curious look. "What? You've been in the office?"

"Where's the flag?" asks Dirk. "Did Billy steal it?"

Piper points at the backpacks next to the flagpole. "Don't worry. It's safe."

Angie rolls up on the bike, all red-faced and angry.

"You chased Billy," says Dirk. "You promised to ignore him."

Angie glances over her shoulder at Billy. "It's hard to ignore a ball hitting my head."

Zane pats Dirk on the back. "Dude, you got sent to the office. We were waiting for you when Billy threw it."

"The office" Angie yells. "And you're telling me how to act!"

Piper <u>fumbles</u> with her notebook. "Uh…these are good lessons to learn," she says. "I think we should make them rules. Raise your hands if you agree. First, don't get in trouble. Second, don't chase Billy."

Four hands shoot into the air.

Piper writes them down:

RULE 1. Don't get sent to the principal's office.
RULE 2. Don't chase Billy.

"We need to vote on somethings else," says Zane. "Put up your hand if you think we should go on *clue journeys* even though everyone can't go."

No one raises their hand, not even Zane.

Dirk has a different idea. "The rule should be… no one goes unless everyone goes."

Zane frowns at him. "We have three weeks to find twelve stars."

Dirk shrugs, like it's no problem. "If we're running out of time, we'll change it."

"That's dumb," says Piper. "I'm not writing down rules that we're just gonna change."

Dirk shoves his hands his pockets. "Okay. Whatever. Sorry I messed up today. It won't happen again."

Piper jots this down. "I'm writing that you <u>apologized</u> for screwing up."

Dirk grimaces. "Why are you writing that down?"

Piper doesn't look up. "I keep detailed notes."

Angie gets off the bike, and says, "I'm sorry that I chased Billy. But I can't promise that it won't happen again. He just…gets on my nerves."

Zane claps his hands. "Tomorrow, we'll meet down at the creek. No one will throw balls at us down there."

FLAGTAG: THE NEW VERB IN TOWN

A hush falls over the classroom. A big hush! Ms. Rae sets a basket covered with a white sheet on a table. Students are on the edge of their seats trying to see what's inside. Ms. Rae likes to bring things to class to teach lessons. Once she brought tadpoles to teach the life cycle of a frog—from spawn to tadpole to froglet. Some students didn't believe the tadpoles were baby frogs until they sprouted arms and legs and hopped away.

Dirk raps his fingers on the desk, thinking about the flag. It'll look just like the white sheet if the StarKids don't find 12 clues soon.

"Time to meet our guest!" Ms. Rae says, lifting the sheet off the cage. "Voila! Meet my friend, Percy."

The students half-stand to see a small pig with a stout body, flat nose, and tiny eyes. It's sniffing the basket and looking around like it's used to 24 kids staring at it.

25

OINK OINK!

Ms. Rae steps up to the front board. "Percy wants to help us learn about nouns and action verbs," she tells the class. "First, who can define a noun?"

Grant raises his hand. "A noun is a person, place, or thing," he says. "In this case, it's Percy the pig!"

"Great answer," says Ms. Rae. "An animal is a noun too. If you can touch, see, hear, smell, or taste it, then it's a noun."

Piper raises her hand, and Ms. Rae gives her *the* nod.

"We can touch, see, hear, smell *and* taste Percy," she says.

"Gross!" cries a girl. "Who would taste Percy?"

Billy <u>leers</u> at the girl. "Duh! Haven't you heard of pigs in a blanket? Or ham sandwiches?"

Angie sits up straight. "That's why I don't eat meat. They kill animals like cows and cute pigs for it."

The classroom goes silent, everyone suddenly hoping for PB&J sandwiches for lunch.

Ms. Rae waves her hands. "Ham! Sandwich!" she exclaims. "These are good examples of nouns!"

"They taste good too," Billy says, loud enough for Angie to hear.

Angie ignores him. She promised herself not to let him bother her. Or at least, not to let him *know* when he's bothering her.

"Let's talk about verbs!" Ms. Rae says, picking up a black marker. "Verbs are action words that describe what someone is doing. Verbs can be physical actions like walking or mental actions like dreaming."

Billy knocks on his desk to get Angie's attention. "Psst. Go eat a cheeseburger."

Angie clenches her fist, telling herself to ignore him. But she can't do it.

"The word *annoy* is a verb," she whispers. "As in you *annoy* everyone."

Billy snickers. He loves Angie's quick comebacks. That's what makes teasing her so much fun.

"Good one," he says. "You crack me up."

Ms. Rae holds out the marker. "I would like everyone to write a verb on the board that describes something that Percy can do. We'll start with the first row."

The students get in line, and one by one write a verb on the board: *eat, roll, burp, grunt, walk, sniff*....

Billy turns around to Piper, slips his hand under his armpit and flaps his arm to make noises. He and Grant crack up.

"Percy farts," he whispers to Piper. "Dare ya to write that verb on the board."

"Don't bother me," says Piper. "I'm busy trying to ignore you."

Billy can't stop laughing. He flaps his arm again. More *fart* noises. More laughter.

Ms. Rae calls the next row. Billy's turn. He writes the word *sweat*.

Ms. Rae watches, curiously. "Interesting word choice," she says. "Why did you pick the word *sweat*?"

"Haven't you heard the saying—*sweats like a pig*?" he asks her.

Ms. Rae takes the marker from him. "Yes, and I find that interesting too because pigs have very few sweat glands. They barely sweat."

Billy rubs his chin. "So, if I tell a guy he sweats like a pig, I'm actually telling him that he doesn't sweat much?"

Grant yells. "Just tell him he sweats like a turkey before Thanksgiving."

The students break into laughter.

When Angie steps up to the board, she writes the word *think*.

"Pigs think," she says. "Unlike some people I know."

Dirk can't focus. He's *thinking* about the U.S. Constitution and whether it might hold a clue. When he found the book on the Constitution, he not only copied pages, he also took notes—

U.S. Constitution

The Constitution is a historic document. It's a plan for how the government should run. It has a bunch of laws too.

Adopted in 1788.

3 years later, they added the first 10 <u>amendments</u> and called them the Bill of Rights.

The First Amendment protects—

1. Freedom of religion—the right to choose my own religion.

2. Freedom of speech—the right to <u>express</u> my opinions.

3. Freedom of <u>press</u>—the right to share my opinions with the media like newspapers, television, radio, and the internet.

4. Freedom of <u>assembly</u>—the right to gather with people in public and protest peacefully.

5. Right to petition the government—this gives people a voice in what happens. We can sign a petition to ask the government to make changes.

Dirk reads his notes over and over, but nothing jumps off the page as a clue. Still, he keeps racking his brain. I got it, he thinks, I'll write a song about the First Amendment. Writing lyrics helps me puzzle out things.

Dirk slips his notes into his pocket, rips a piece of paper from a notebook and writes:

Dude,

When we know the state we're flagtagging to, we should learn as much as possible about it before we go. It might help us find the clue. I researched the U.S. Constitution. The Declaration of Independence was written and signed in Pennsylvania too. Can you research it?

He taps Zane's shoulder and shows him the note. Zane doesn't want to take it because if Ms. Rae sees Dirk passing notes, he could get a detention. He grabs it anyway, reads it over, and underlines the verbs.

Dude,

When we <u>know</u> the state we're <u>flagtagging</u> to, we should <u>learn</u> as much as possible about it before we <u>go</u>. It might <u>help</u> us <u>find</u> the clue. I <u>researched</u> the U.S. Constitution. The Declaration of Independence was <u>written</u> and <u>signed</u> in Pennsylvania too. Can you <u>research</u> it?

On the bottom, Zane writes STOP PASSING NOTES and slips it back to Dirk.

When Dirk sees it, a big smile spreads across his face. "You underlined *flagtagging*," he whispers. "Cool! We have our own secret verb."

CHAPTER
Five

COUNTDOWN UNTIL SHOWTIME!

F*lagtag* time! Pennsylvania time!

Zane, Dirk, and Piper are at the creek ready to go. Only, one thing is missing. Angie! She's five minutes late.

Piper has the <u>heebie-jeebies</u>. <u>Venturing</u> into the unknown is not her thing. And she's worried about Angie too. If she doesn't show up soon, the StarKids can't go. Another day wasted.

It's so <u>nerve-racking</u>!

Zane is even more stressed out. He's just better at hiding it, quietly tossing rocks in the creek. But he's worried about *everything*. *Flagtagging* to Pennsylvania. Another delay. Not going. Or worse, never going!

Dirk's totally fine, eager to leave. Sitting on a tree branch, he leans back, hangs upside down, and sees the magic flag spilling out of his backpack. "I bet this old flag has seen a lot of things," he remarks. "Do you think it was around during the American Revolutionary War?"

"If it was," says Zane, "it only had 13 stars." He throws the last of his rocks and wipes his hands on his jeans. "By the way, I researched the Declaration of Independence."

"Oh yeah!" says Dirk. "What did you learn?"

"It goes back to the first 13 British colonies," Zane tells him, "when the Patriots were fighting England for independence."

"Wait!" Piper sits on a log and takes her notebook out of her backpack. "Okay. Go ahead."

Zane jumps right in. "King George III bullied the colonists. If they didn't follow his orders, he'd send his army to make them. The Patriots wanted to break from England so, they went to war…the American Revolutionary War."

"Slow down!" Piper says, writing it all down. "I'm calling it—ARW."

When Piper looks up, Zane continues. "Thomas Jefferson and other Patriots wrote the Declaration of Independence."

"Stop right there!" says Piper. "*Declaration of Independence* takes too long to write. I'm shortening it to DOI."

Dirk has a big upside-down grin on his face. "When we talk about this stuff, we'll use those <u>acronyms</u> and have our own secret code."

Zane nods. "The DOI lists the unfair things the king did to the colonists and explains why they <u>rebelled</u>. Get this! It was like an announcement telling the world that the 13 colonies were now one country called the United States of America."

"Wow," says Piper. "The Patriots declared independence before they'd even won the war. Now, that's gutsy. I think—."

A voice interrupts her. "What's up, StarKids?"

Angie's on the bank, strolling down the path in a hot pink astronaut costume and a space helmet with her skateboard strapped into her backpack.

Dirk pulls himself up onto the branch. "Yay! Time to blast off!"

Zane takes one look at her, and yelps, "It's about time. Let's go!!!!"

DID MY HEAD GET BIGGER OR WHAT?

Angie reaches them, tries to take off her helmet but it's too tight, so Piper helps pry it off.

"Sorry I'm late," she says. "Today was *fish day*?"

"Fish day?" asks Piper. "What does *that* mean?"

Angie looks around for a place to hide the helmet. "Remember the aquarium in Mr. Weber's classroom? He has new fish, Nemo and Dory. I feed them once a week after school."

Dirk jumps down from the branch. "Why are you wearing an astronaut costume?"

"Who are you supposed to be?" asks Zane. "Neil Armstrong?"

"Is he one of those billionaires who fly into space for fun?" asks Angie.

"No," says Zane. "He was the first person to walk on the moon."

"Oh, that guy," Angie says, stashing her helmet behind a bush. "He wore a white astronaut spacesuit. Not pink."

36

"Did you know that Neil A backward spells Alien?" asks Dirk.

"No way!" says Zane. "That's too funny."

Piper eyes Angie's skateboard. "Are you taking that?"

"If it doesn't go, I don't go," Angie tells her.

All this waiting is making Zane hungry. He takes a baggie out of his backpack, and asks, "Anyone want a chocolate chip cookie before we go? Mom's special recipe."

"What makes it so special?" asks Dirk.

"Caramel," says Zane. "And macadamia nuts."

"Who thinks Angie should get to take her skateboard?" asks Dirk. "If you vote *yes,* you'll get a cookie."

Four hands fly up.

Piper writes in her notebook:

RULE 3: Angie can bring her skateboard.

Everyone reaches into the baggie for a cookie.

"Should we take anything else?" asks Piper, "like a first aid kit?"

Dirk shrugs. "Nope. We're good."

Piper looks Angie up and down. "Your costume might draw attention. Maybe you should hide it with the helmet."

Zane crams the baggie into his backpack. "No one will notice it," he says. "I didn't until Dirk said something."

Piper looks at him, curiously. How could he not notice a pink astronaut costume? Angie sticks out like Waldo once you've found him.

Dirk asks Angie what she discovered when she researched Pennsylvania. "You won't believe this," she says. "The Crayola Factory is there! It makes three billion crayons a year. That's nine million a day."

"Really!" says Dirk. "Nine million a day?"

"Yeah!" replies Angie. "And the Philadelphia Zoo is the first public zoo in America."

"Good work," says Piper. "I'll write that down."

Zane had hoped to hear about historic sites and landmarks. Not crayons and zoos.

"Did you read anything about the historical sites?" he asks her.

"Why?" asks Angie. "Just because we're going to Pennsylvania doesn't mean the clue has something to do with history. We could find it swinging with the gorillas at America's first zoo."

"Guys," says Piper. "We gotta go."

Dirk sets his backpack on the ground, and without a word, they all reach in and tag the flag with both hands….

ROCK AND STEEL RULE

F lashing lights! Blasting music! It's an amphitheater.

The StarKids are on a stage with a heavy metal band looking out at an audience, a big blur of bright colors. People are packed in like sardines, singing to the music and boogeying to the beat.

Dirk's fired up, clapping and stomping. "Let's get this party started!"

Zane's frozen. He can't wrap his brain around it: Creek. Concert. He covers his ears. But the beat goes on: Creek. Concert. Creek. Concert.

Piper's watching the people in front of the stage hop up and down and punch their fists in the air.

It's a new dance, she thinks. *Hit hop!*

Angie's tapping her feet and taking it all in when she spots a modern glass building across the street. It's surrounded by old brick warehouses with rusty steel roofs and boarded-up windows. The glass building looks out of place, sort of like a swan swimming with a raft of ducks.

Piper leans into Angie's ear. "Do you think we're invisible?" she shouts. "No one seems to see us."

Angie starts to the front of the stage. "Come on! We have a clue to find."

Piper tugs on Zane's sleeve. "Hey! Time to leave!"

He shakes himself. "Huh? Yeah. Okay."

The StarKids jump off the stage, squeeze around the *hit hoppers* and dash up a path to a brick road. Angie tosses down her skateboard and bounces over the bumpy brick road while Dirk, Piper, and Zane chase after her.

"Wait!" yells Zane. "We need a plan."

When Angie reaches the entryway to the glass building, she glances back at them.

"We don't have time to plan," she says. "We need to look for the—"

Her mouth drops open. And her eyes get wide.

"What the heck?" she gasps, staring at something behind them. "What's that?"

Zane, Piper, and Dirk whirl around to see a jungle of steel—furnaces, smokestacks, beams, ladders, and pipes—<u>looming</u> over the stage. It looks like something out of a horror movie.

They've never seen anything like it.

Piper takes off her glasses, wipes the smudgy lenses on her shirt and puts them back on. "Looks like a grounded ship."

"Or city in outer space," says Zane.

"Good thing I wore my astronaut costume!" Angie says, turning for the door. "Let's check this place out."

The lobby of the glass building is two stories high. A counter in front of them has flat screen televisions on the wall behind it. Tables and chairs are scattered about. In the far corner, a bright orange metal staircase leads up to a second level. Above them is a ceiling with bright orange metal rafters, pipes, and beams.

"What's orange and sounds like a parrot?" asks Dirk.

"A carrot," replies Zane. "I know that joke."

"Guys," says Angie. "Get serious! Focus."

The door closes behind them and it's suddenly quiet.

A bald man is sitting at a table next to the door eating a hamburger and french fries.

One whiff of the beef and Dirk's searching for a food <u>vendor</u>. The place is closed, he thinks. So, why's the man in here? And where'd he get the food?

"Hi. What is this place?" Zane asks the man.

"The ArtsQuest Center," he replies. "You're at the old Bethlehem Steel <u>Plant</u>."

The StarKids stare out the huge window at the monstrosity behind the stage.

"That thing is a steel plant?" asks Zane. "Are you sure?"

The man tosses a french fry in his mouth. "I worked in it for 53 years until it closed."

"Looks scary," says Angie. "Was it dangerous working in there?"

The old man glances out at the plant with a faraway look in his eyes. "Hundreds of men died in there…thousands were injured." He pauses. "I almost fell into a fire once, but my buddy grabbed me…and saved my life."

"Sounds awful," says Dirk. "Why'd you work in there?"

The old man looks at him. "You could say steel runs in my blood," he says. "My father, brothers and I worked in the plant, so did many other families. It was our <u>livelihood</u>."

"What sort of things did you make in there?" asks Zane. "Planes and ships?"

"Everything big!" says the man, "We even built parts for famous landmarks like the Empire State Building and Golden Gate Bridge."

Something catches Angie's eye, a shadow on the second level. She can see it through the glass railing. She rubs her eyes and it fades into the lights.

Phew, I imagined it, she thinks. Talk about spooky!

Piper points out at the huge cylinder-shaped tanks. "What are those things?"

The man doesn't look out the window. "Blast furnaces," he replies. "We'd boil iron ore and other materials in those furnaces and turn it into pig iron. Then, we'd <u>refine</u> the pig iron to make steel."

Piper's eyes light up. "How hot did they get?"

"Over 2000 degrees Fahrenheit. Hot enough to turn *anything* into liquid."

Zane feels a lump in his throat. "*Anything?* Yikes!"

"Why is the plant still here?" asks Zane. "Why didn't they tear it down?"

The man picks up his hamburger, and says, "it's an important part of this town. The city <u>preserved</u> it out of respect for its history. Thousands of <u>immigrants</u> moved here to work in the plant and many of those families are still here today."

"Immigrants?" asks Dirk. "Are those people who come to live in America?"

The man nods and bites into his hamburger. "In the late 1800s and early 1900s, immigrants from around the world came to this country. That's why America was called a *melting pot*. It's a <u>metaphor</u>. It means that people came here from countries with different cultures, *melted together*...and created an American identity."

Piper imagines Americans flocking into the steel mill wearing the same yellow hard hats and carrying the same silver lunch boxes. But everyone looks totally different.

"America doesn't seem like a *melting pot* to me," she remarks. "When you *melt* things together, you get one substance, like the things *melted* in those furnaces to make pig iron. But people don't just *melt* together and become the same."

46

Dirk eyes the man's hamburger, the beef patty dripping with <u>condiments</u> like mustard, mayonnaise, ketchup, and relish.

"America seems more like a hamburger," he says. "The beef is our country, and the condiments are the people who give it flavor."

Angie rolls her eyes. "Why is everything about food with you?"

The man can't help but smile. "Dirk, I like that metaphor," he says, chewing his hamburger. "You're saying that people keep their own unique identities."

Dirk gives him a funny look. "Uh…yeah. Sure."

"And the bun binds us together," adds Zane. "It's our American culture."

Dirk grins at Angie. "See! I'm not the only one who sees America as a big hamburger."

Suddenly, Dirk lights up like a glow-in-the dark toy.

"Do something," Piper whispers. "Make it stop."

Dirk gives her a dirty look. How's he supposed to stop it. He doesn't know why it's glowing.

"Umm…gotta go," he says, backing out the door. "Nice talking to you."

Angie hears a strange noise. The shadow! It's floating down the orange staircase! She freaks out and grabs Piper's arm.

"Time to leave," she says, tugging her to the exit. "Have a nice hamburger. I mean…uh…day."

Outside, Dirk is knelt on the concrete staring down at his glowing backpack.

"I think the flag's trying to tell us something," he says. "Maybe it wants to go home."

"That was super weird," says Piper. "Dirk looked like a glow stick and the man didn't seem to notice."

"That's not all," adds Zane. "He called Dirk by his name. How'd he know it?"

Angie doesn't mention the spooky shadow. They have a bigger problem, a flag that won't stop glowing.

The StarKids hurry behind a small white building and huddle around the backpack. When Dirk opens it, the light's so bright, everyone shields their eyes.

"Tag it now while it's lit up," says Dirk.

The StarKids quickly reach into the backpack and tag the flag.…

KEEP AN EYE ON THE SKY

Woohoo! On bikes in a brick-paved alley, they can hear a city grumbling around them. Honking horns. Screaming sirens. And the *whir* of a nearby freeway.

"We learned something," yells Dirk. "The flag glows when it's time to leave."

"Yeah, but we didn't have time to look for a clue," says Zane.

"What city is this?" shouts Piper. "Look for signs."

Angie can still see the shadow moving toward her. Ghosts don't exist, she tells herself.

She tries to pull up on the handlebars to do a wheelie, but the front tire won't lift off the ground. The handlebars won't move either. She slams the brake. The bike won't slow down or speed up.

"I can't control this bike," she cries.

Piper, Zane, and Dirk try, but they can't steer or change speeds either.

"They're taking us somewhere," yells Zane. "Where?"

A jogger turns down the alley. She's staring down at the brick road unaware that she's on a collision course with four runaway bikes.

"Watch out!" Dirk yells to her. "We're going to crash!"

The jogger doesn't look up.

"Hey!" yells Zane. "Get out of the way. We can't stop!"

Dirk yanks the handlebar with all his force.

His bike swerves up onto the sidewalk and almost collides into a wooden planter. When he glances back, Zane, Piper and Angie are still behind him, their eyes as big as binoculars. Once the jogger runs by, the bikes jump from the sidewalk back onto the brick road.

"Whoa," says Angie. "That was gnarly."

Something in the sky casts a dark shadow over the bikes. Zane glances up and sees a bald eagle with its wings spread out.

"Is that *Lucy*?" he shouts.

The others tilt their heads back. An eagle is soaring overhead drilling them with angry eyes as if it's hunting for prey.

"That's not Lucy," cries Angie. "She doesn't look so evil!"

The eagle hovers above Dirk, then swoops down and digs its sharp talons into his backpack. Dirk tries to stop the bike, but he can't.

"Get off me!" he yells. "Get away!"

The eagle flaps its wings and tears at his backpack with its beak. Dirk twists around and swats at it. Zane and Angie try to speed up, but the bikes won't go faster.

"Hit it!" screams Angie. "Make it let go!"

"What do you think I'm doing!" yells Dirk.

The eagle finally releases the backpack and lifts into the air.

"Do you have food in your backpack?" asks Zane. "Any candy?"

"Eagles don't eat junk food," Piper hollers. "They eat things like fish and squirrels."

"No fish or squirrels in my backpack," shouts Dirk.

The eagle flies up to a rooftop and perches on a chimney, then looks down at them, all proud and mighty.

"I think it's after the magic flag," yells Angie.

"Why would it want a flag?" asks Zane. "Maybe it's just a mama protecting her nest."

"Eagles don't live in cities," says Piper. "They like to build their nests near lakes or oceans where there's food."

"How do you know so much about bald eagles?" he asks her.

"I did a report on them," replies Piper. "The bald eagle is our national bird."

As the StarKids near the end of the alley, they see vehicles zipping by on a crossroad.

"Cars!" cries Angie. "We need to bail."

Everyone glances down at the brick road. Jump? Yikes!

"Ready?" yells Angie. "On three! One…two…"

Just as they're about to jump, the bikes slow down. No one says a word as they roll around a corner onto a sidewalk and glide alongside a brick wall under a <u>canopy</u> of trees.

Zane feels his bike wobble. "We're stopping!"

They come to an intersection where <u>pedestrians</u> are waiting for the light to change. There's a fire station across the street and a huge mural on the side of a building.

"Welcome to Philadelphia," a voice calls. "Isn't it a great city!"

The StarKids spot Lucy in one of the sidewalk trees. The collage of bright colors is hard to miss. She looks like a rainbow gone wrong, <u>decked out</u> in an orange blouse, red tights, green shoes, blue cap, and a yellow wig. She likes to glam up on trips to the city.

"Was the bike ride fun?" she asks. "I tried to get you closer to the *clue site* but…well...let's just say, I had some <u>technical difficulties</u>."

The StarKids look really confused. Even Lucy notices it and she's no expert at reading human faces.

"Did I mention that you'll visit three *clue sites* in each state?" she asks them.

"What are *clue sites*?" asks Piper. "Places we look for clues?"

Lucy bobs her head up and down. "You got it."

"We didn't have enough time to look for a clue at the steel plant," Angie complains.

Lucy lets out a screechy snort. "Objection! Not true. Think about all the things you saw and heard."

The StarKids go quiet. Thinking back, they did see and hear a lot.

"An eagle attacked me!" blurts Dirk. "It tried to get in my backpack!"

Lucy waves a wing. "Ah. That's just George."

"George!" cries Dirk. "Why's he trying to steal it?"

"Well...he wants the flag."

"Why?" asks Piper. "Does he know it's magic?"

"Actually...it's his flag." Lucy grinds her beak. "Listen, we can talk later. You need to get to the Friends meeting house."

Zane hasn't said a word. Hearing about Lucy is one thing, seeing her *in full color* is another.

Lucy lowers her head and peers at him. "Zane, we haven't met," she says, sweetly. "Is there anything I can do for you?"

Zane stumbles over his words. "Thank...no... you."

"Good!" Lucy squawks. "Get moving! You're late for a Quaker meeting!"

Piper takes out her notebook. "Quaker meeting?" she mumbles, searching for a pen. "You said the *Friends* meeting house."

"Same! Same!" Lucy waves her head up and down. "Quakers are members of the Religious Society of Friends. It's a religion."

Piper writes in her notebook: Quakers are also known as Friends.

"You don't have time to take notes!" Lucy shrieks. "Go!"

"Okay," says Piper. "But why are we going to a Quaker meeting?"

"Dunno," says Lucy. "Maybe it's because William Penn, the man who founded Pennsylvania, was a Quaker. He came here from England to start a free colony where people could join any church they wanted."

The StarKids stare at her blankly.

"What are you talking about?" asks Angie.

Lucy groans and claws at her beak. "I thought I told you this already," she squawks. "Many British settlers came to America for religious freedom. The king wanted everyone to join the Church of England. People like the Quakers who had other beliefs were punished. So, it was big deal when Penn founded a colony where people could choose their religion."

"I get it," says Dirk, leaning his bike against the brick wall. "Come on. We don't want to be late."

The StarKids dump the bikes, dash around the corner and through a gateway. The meeting house has a pitched roof, two yellow doors and several windows, some with shutters. Angie stops on the brick driveway to take out her skateboard.

"Why didn't Lucy warn us about George?" she asks, curiously. "What else is she hiding from us?"

No one...says...a word.

CHAPTER
Eight

TO REALLY HEAR, YOU GOTTA LISTEN

The lobby of the Arch Street Meeting House is plain. No decorations. No artwork. No frills. And no furniture except for a reception desk inside the front door.

There's no one around either. It's super quiet.

"We need a signal for when we see that mean eagle, George," says Zane.

"I'm just gonna scream as loud as I can," Angie tells him.

They wander into a <u>dimly</u> lit museum the size of a small gym. The walls are covered with posters, articles, and photographs of men in big, black hats and women in bonnets.

Angie glances around and walks back out. "I'm gonna find the meeting."

58

She moves <u>swiftly</u> through the lobby, stops at a set of double doors and tugs on the handles. The doors are locked. She listens for voices, but hears nothing.

Too quiet, she thinks. No meeting in there. She spots another door on the far side of the lobby, tosses down her skateboard and zooms toward it.

Meanwhile, in the museum, Zane and Piper are reading articles about the Quakers while Dirk tries to figure out whether a sketch is meant to be serious or <u>comical</u>. The Quaker man has a straight face, but he's wearing an overcoat with tight shorts and high socks.

HERO BEFORE HIS TIME
Benjamin Lay

RIGHT IS RIGHT
EVEN IF EVERYONE IS AGAINST IT

WRONG IS WRONG
EVEN IF EVERYONE IS FOR IT.
—WILLIAM PENN

Dirk wonders if men even wore shorts 150 years ago. Maybe it's underwear, he thinks. Now, if he was in *tighty whities*, I'd know it was meant to be funny.

"Whoa," says Piper. "Lucy told us that British people were punished if they didn't join the Church of England. This article says that William Penn went to prison for being a Quaker."

"It's interesting that the colonists could choose their religion in America," says Zane. "The king of England controlled the colonies. He obviously gave them a little more freedom."

"Not enough," says Piper. "Remember, lotsa colonists felt the king wasn't fair. That's why the Patriots fought in the American Revolutionary War…ARW…to get away from England."

Dirk starts toward them. "No one forgot King George III," he says. "Even after America broke from England, people worried that the new government would act like him and take away their freedoms." Dirk reaches into his pocket. "That's why they added the Bill of Rights to the U.S. Constitution...it protects those freedoms."

Piper and Zane stare at Dirk in disbelief. Is this the Dirk they know? Talking about the Constitution? And the Bill of Rights?

Dirk smiles proudly. "I took some notes." He takes a crinkled piece of paper out of his pocket and shows it to them.

U.S. Constitution

The Constitution is a historic document. It's a plan for how the government should run. It has a bunch of laws too.

Adopted in 1788.

3 years later, they added the first 10 <u>amendments</u> and called them the Bill of Rights.

The First Amendment protects—

1. Freedom of religion—the right to choose my own religion.
2. Freedom of speech—the right to <u>express</u> my opinions.
3. Freedom of <u>press</u>—the right to share my opinions with the media like newspapers, television, radio, and the internet.
4. Freedom of <u>assembly</u>—the right to gather with people in public and protest peacefully.
5. Right to petition the government—this gives people a voice in what happens. We can sign a petition to ask the government to make changes.

By the time Piper and Zane finish reading the notes, their mouths are open so wide, their jaws almost touch the floor. They've never seen this side of Dirk. He's never shown much interest in history. What's up?

Dirk slips his notes into his pocket. "Why are you looking at me like that?" he asks. "We need to learn this stuff to bring the stars home. I even wrote a song about the First Amendment. Want to hear it?"

"Maybe later," says Zane. "First, let's find the clue."

In the lobby, Angie glides across the floor on her skateboard, kicks it up, opens the door and listens.

It's quiet. Completely quiet.

No meeting in here either, she thinks.

But when she peeks inside, she's stunned by what she sees: a big room full of people!

"No one's talking," she mumbles to herself. "What's going on? Are they hypnotized or something?"

Angie waits for someone to speak. Nothing happens. Everyone just sits there. It's as if they're playing the *silent* game and they're *super* good at it!

She closes the door and hurries to the museum.

So many weird things have happened, she thinks. Spooky shadow. Runaway bikes. Evil eagle. And now silent people. Strange!

In the museum, Piper is reading a Notice of Trial.

"Susan B. Anthony was a Quaker who was arrested for illegally voting in a presidential election," she says. "I wonder what she did wrong."

AN
ACCOUNT OF THE PROCEEDINGS
ON THE
TRIAL OF
SUSAN B. ANTHONY
ON THE
Charge of Illegal Voting
AND ON THE
TRIAL OF
BEVERLY W. JONES, EDWIN T. MARSH
AND WILLIAM B. HALL,

Zane makes a face, a sort of squinty face. "She voted," he tells her. "Things weren't equal back then. Only men could vote. It was a crime for women to vote."

Piper studies a sketch of Susan B. Anthony. "Why would she vote if she knew it was a crime?"

"She stood up for what she believed in," says Zane. "Susan B. Anthony was a famous <u>activist</u> who fought for women's rights."

"Looks like a lot of Quaker activists fought for equal rights," Dirk says, scanning the walls.

oo WOW! I HAVE A LOT OF WORK TO DO!

"They fought to <u>abolish</u> slavery too." He reads a caption under a photograph. "Quakers respect people's differences and see everyone as equal."

HOW DO YOU STAND UP FOR SOMETHING YOU BELIEVE IN?

Angie rushes into the museum, puffing and <u>panting</u>.

"I found the meeting," she <u>gasps</u>. "It's so weird. Tons of people are inside a room, but no one's talking."

Angie beckons to them. "Hurry. Come with me!"

Piper, Zane, and Dirk follow her through the lobby trying to imagine a *silent* meeting. Impossible. How would they get anything done if no one talks? But when they get to the meeting, that's exactly what they find. People sitting in silence.

Absolute silence!

Zane scratches his head. "Maybe they're <u>meditating</u>."

"Could the word silence be the clue?" Piper whispers. "Lucy told us to focus on what we see and hear. And right now, we hear *silence*."

"The first clue was a word," Angie reminds them. "It was *perseverance*. Remember? It's a person's ability to keep trying even when things get really tough."

Zane scratches his head. "Maybe that's why Lucy told us to pay attention to what people say and do. The clue could be a word that describes a skill or how someone acts or thinks."

"Exactly," says Angie. "Like the first clue."

Dirk <u>shifts</u> from one foot to the other. "My head's gonna burst from all this silence. Can we leave?"

Passing through the lobby, the StarKids notice a lady behind the reception desk reading a novel. Her long brown hair is pulled back in a ponytail and her blue-framed glasses match her blouse.

Dirk nudges Zane in the arm. "Looks like Quakers wear normal clothes," he whispers.

"What did you expect?" Zane asks him. "Bonnets and big, black hats?"

Dirk thinks about this. "Yeah. Pretty much."

Angie marches up to the reception desk and stops in front of the lady. "Hi...uh...we noticed that the meeting is sorta quiet."

Piper, Zane, and Dirk step in next to her. The lady looks up over the rim of her glasses and gives them a warm smile.

"Meetings for worship are very quiet," she replies. "We don't have <u>sermons</u>. No one speaks unless someone wants to share a message. Then, we sit quietly and think about it."

Dirk can't imagine this. "What if no one shares a message? Do you just sit there the whole time?"

The lady's eyes smile at him. "We believe everyone has a light within...," she explains. "When we worship, we focus on that inner light."

The StarKids gaze at her. No one says a word.

The lady glances at each of them. "Think about it," she says. "To really hear, you have to listen."

Zane motions to Piper. "Write that down. It sounds important."

Piper looks at him, curiously. "You want me to write down: 'to hear, you gotta listen?' Isn't that obvious?"

Zane shrugs. "Not really. Some people don't listen. Look at Dirk!"

Dirk doesn't hear Zane. He isn't listening. He's too busy thinking.

"Why would Lucy want us to go to a silent meeting?" he asks. "How's it gonna help us find the clue?"

Zane bites his lower lip. He doesn't think they should mention the clue around people.

It's a secret mission!

"We need to add another rule," he says. "Don't talk about the *clue* unless we're alone."

Piper raises her pen. "I'm writing that instead of the stuff about listening."

She jots down:

RULE 4: Don't talk about the clue in front of people.

There's a flash of light! Dirk's backpack suddenly looks like it's full of glow-in-the-dark balls. Everyone freezes.

The lady swivels toward him. "What's in your backpack?"

Piper is quick to answer. "Actually…it's sort of a signal. It tells us when it's time to leave."

The lady lets out a hearty laugh. "Great idea!

When I was a kid, mothers rang cow bells to call us home. Some kids would pretend not to hear them so they could play outside longer. But no one could pretend not to see that bright light."

The glowing flag starts to flash like someone's flipping an on-off switch. Dirk panics, slips out the front door and runs around the side of the house. By the time they find him, the flashing light has lost its shine. It's fading.

"What's goin' on?" cries Zane "Is it losing power?"

"It runs on magic," Piper tells him. "Not Triple A batteries!"

Dirk reaches into his backpack, takes out a section of the flag for everyone to tag and looks at Zane.

"Dude," he says. "Don't doubt the magic!"

CHAPTER
Nine

MAKIN' MUSICAL MEMORIES

It's cold, freezing cold. And pitch black too. The StarKids can't see a thing, but they can hear the *clicks*, *hums* and *whirs* of nearby machines.

"Guys," whispers Angie. "Where are you?"

"Right here," Zane replies, squinting into the darkness. "Are we in a closet?"

"I'm here too," says Dirk. "Where's Piper?"

A door opens. Noise streams in. An overhead light comes on.

Angie, Zane, and Dirk are standing between a wall and stack of boxes. But Piper's not with them!

They inch quietly along the wall and peek out into a warehouse at huge shelves stuffed with boxes, containers, tools, and equipment. A woman enters the warehouse, grabs a brown bag off a table and hurries out, leaving the lights on. Angie, Zane, and Dirk step out from behind the boxes glancing around.

"Piper," Angie calls out. "Are you here?"

"Up here," comes a shaky voice. "See me?"

They track the voice up toward the ceiling. Piper's sitting on the top shelf waving at them.

Zane sighs. "We need to get her down before someone else comes in."

Dirk scans the shelves. "There has to be a ladder around here somewhere," he says.

He spots a big wooden cart against a wall.

Bingo!

They run to get it and roll it directly below Piper.

"Okay," says Dirk. "Jump on this."

There's a moment of tense silence as Piper stares down at the cart. Everyone is plain worried. Worried that Piper won't jump. Worried that she will. She could hurt herself!

Piper feels the color drain out of her face. "Uh...what if I fall?"

Angie crosses her arms and yells, "You won't! Jump and squat down like a cat."

"Cats have nine lives," says Piper. "I only have one."

"Speaking of cats," says Dirk. "What's the difference between a cat and a frog?"

Angie scowls at him. "We don't have time for stupid jokes."

Dirk ignores her. "A cat has nine lives, but a frog croaks every day."

Thud! Thump! Bam!

They whirl around to Piper crouched on top of the cart. She stands up, tosses her hair back and throws her hands out.

"I'm not just *any* cat," she says, smiling. "Call me Cougar!"

Angie, Dirk, and Zane move in around the cart
and help her down.

"Do you think we're still in Pennsylvania?"
asks Angie.

"Who knows?" says Zane. "With the way Lucy
keeps messing up, we could be anywhere."

They open the door to a buzzing factory
and start along a walkway between rows of
workstations. Dirk stops when he sees a robotic
arm pressing a guitar against a power sander.

"A guitar factory!" he yelps. "No way!"

Suddenly, guitars are everywhere: on
tables, shelves and hanging from racks. At one

workstation, a woman is <u>clamping</u> the frame of a guitar together while a man across from her is clipping giant clothes pins on one.

"Welcome to C.F. Martin and Company," someone says.

A bearded man with light brown hair is standing behind them.

"Martins!" exclaims Dirk. "I have an old Martin's guitar. My mom bought it at a garage sale."

The man raises his eyebrows. "How old? It could be valuable."

Dirk's face lights up. Mom scored when she bought the old bucket, he thinks. The magic flag was on the bottom. Maybe she scored with the old guitar too.

"Are we in Pennsylvania?" asks Angie.

"Yes," says the man. "We've been headquartered here since Christian Martin founded this company in 1833."

"The steel plant started here too," says Piper. "Maybe the clue has something to do—."

Oops! She just broke Rule 4. No talking about the *clue* in front of people.

Zane clears his throat. "Hey! I think it's neat that robotic machines and people work together in here."

The man explains that the robots speed up different processes. "But we'll always need our employees to do the tasks that require skill and precision," he adds.

Dirk knows that guitar stores usually let people try out guitars, and asks, "Do you have demo guitars?"

"In the lobby," says the man. "You're welcome to try them."

Dirk really, really wants to demo some cool guitars. But he'd have to get to the lobby and back before the magic flag lights up.

At the next station, a woman slips a sheet of wood into a press machine.

"Once the wood is completely flat," says the man. "It moves to the next station where the laser machine cuts it into the shape of a guitar."

"This is an assembly line!" exclaims Piper. "The guitars move from station to station. At each station, they add something or do different work until the guitar is completely put together. Right?"

"Exactly," replies the man. "Each worker does an operation, then passes it on to the next worker who performs another operation. It takes over 300 operations to fully assemble one guitar."

"Most things are made on an assembly line," Zane tells them. "It was invented in America."

"Skateboards were invented in America too," Angie chimes in. "Surfers invented them. On the days they couldn't surf the waves, they'd attach roller skates to boards and cruise the streets. Cool, huh?"

Dirk spots a sign to the lobby. He can't ignore it. He really wants to demo a few guitars. The next thing he knows, he's <u>hightailing</u> it through the factory.

The lobby is large with a museum, souvenir shop, and room with demo guitars. Dirk goes straight for the guitars, lifts one off the wall and starts playing a song he wrote—You Smelt It. You Dealt It. He doesn't sing the lyrics though. He doesn't want to get kicked out.

In the factory, Zane, Piper, and Angie watch a laser machine burn lines into a piece of wood. Two women are at the machine. One is a tall brunette, and the other, a short redhead.

"I forgot to ask for time off," says the brunette. "I won't be able to go to the charity event."

"You've worked so hard on it," says the redhead. "I won't let you miss it. I'll work for you."

"Really?" asks the brunette. "Are you sure?"

"Positive!"

"Thank you. You're the best."

"You're welcome."

Zane tugs on Piper's sleeve, and whispers, "The employees in here are so polite."

Angie notices that Dirk is gone. She looks up and down the walkway but can't see him anywhere.

"Where's Dirk?" she asks. "Did he leave?"

"He mentioned demo guitars," replies Zane. "I bet he went to the lobby."

"Just follow the signs," says the man.

Zane, Piper, and Angie find the lobby and even the guitar room, but not Dirk. He's nowhere in sight.

"Let's split up and look for him," suggests Zane. "He could be anywhere."

Piper glimpses a bright light streaming out from under a door and recognizes it at once.

"It's the magic flag!" she blurts. "Time to go home!"

They race past the hanging guitars, push open the door and startle Dirk who's standing in a hallway with his glowing backpack. When he sees them, he <u>heaves</u> a sigh of relief.

"You scared me," he gasps. "I thought—"

"What are you doing?" cries Piper. "Why'd you ditch us?"

"I was playing a guitar when the flag lit up," he replies. "I was coming back to find you."

"Playing a guitar?" Angie yelps. "You left—"

Zane interrupts. "Guys, we need to leave."

Dirk throws opens his backpack, and the others gather around the light and reach inside....

CHAPTER
Ten

KNOW THE CODE!

"Where are we?" asks Angie. "We're supposed to be at the creek. Something went wrong."

The wood-paneled room is symmetrical. Split down the middle, each half would mirror the other. There's a desk at the back, and on each side of it, an identical fireplace, door, and side wall with three identical windows.

"Lucy must've added another *clue site*," says Dirk. "But why?"

Zane studies the room: white and gray paneled walls, wooden chairs, green table clothes. It looks familiar. He's seen it before. Where?

"History books," he howls. "I think we're in Independence Hall. This is where it *all* happened!"

"Can you be a little more specific?" asks Piper. "What all happened?"

"This is where America was born," Zane tells her. "The delegates signed the DOI here during the ARW."

Dirk smiles so wide, his cheeks dimple. DOI. ARW. The secret code is awesome!

"Huh? Clue me in," says Angie. This is her *cool* way of asking what they're talking about.

"The DOI is the Declaration of Independence," Piper tells her. "We talked about a secret code while you were feeding fish."

Angie can tell by Piper's tone of voice that she's still mad at her for showing up to the creek late.

"I promised Mr. Weber I'd feed Nemo and Dory," she says, calmly. "I don't break my promises."

"But you promised us that you'd be on time," says Piper. "That didn't happen."

Angie thinks this through. She *did* make that promise. And she was late.

"Hmm…I'm sorry," she says. "I didn't think of it that way. Is there a word that means to *overpromise*? That's what I did."

That's the thing about Angie; she admits when she's wrong and apologizes too.

"Yeah," says Piper. "The word is literally *overpromise*."

There's a scuffing noise at back of the room. A tall man with a gray wig and serious face appears in a doorway. He's wearing a soldier uniform from the American Revolution War: a long blue wool coat, gold waistcoat, breeches, and black boots. His wig is ridiculously cool, high on top with waves that curl above his ears.

Dirk bursts out laughing. "Nice costume!" he says. "Let me guess. You're Thomas Jefferson, the guy who wrote the Declaration of Independence."

The man doesn't crack a smile. "George Washington," he replies, gruffly. "First president of the United States."

"And the Commander-in-Chief of the Continental Army during the ARW," says Zane. "You fought the British army, the most powerful army in the world…and won!"

"We'll call you GW," laughs Dirk. "I like how the tour guides here dress up like historical figures."

GW sits down at the desk. "Welcome to the Assembly Room," he says, flatly. "Do you have any questions?"

The StarKids push through a gate and move to the back. Up close, GW's blue eyes look tired. His uniform is wrinkled and worn, and his boots are scuffed-up. He smells old, musty like Ole Magic.

"Was George Washington here on July 4th, 1776, when they signed the Declaration of Independence?" Zane asks him.

"No." GW stares up at a crystal chandelier. "I was fighting in the American Revolutionary War at the time. But I was here when we wrote the U.S. Constitution. Delegates from twelve colonies crammed into this room for over four months."

"I thought leaders from all thirteen colonies came to the convention," says Zane.

GW rubs his chin. "Rhode Island didn't send a delegate," he says. "We had plans to create a stronger federal government. The people of Rhode Island didn't want a federal government with too much power."

Dirk points his index fingers at GW. "Ahha! They were afraid the government would take away their special rights."

GW's eyes soften. "'Tis a fact. They worried that a strong federal government would control the states and interfere with individual freedoms. Later, we added the Bill of Rights to the Constitution to protect those individual rights."

"I wrote a rap song about the First Amendment," Dirk says, excitedly. "It's called, *Ode to G Dub and the delegate dudes*. Want to hear it?"

GW looks puzzled. "Rap? No. Not particularly."

Dirk taps a foot and snaps his fingers, then bursts into song,

> *"Let's talk about the First Amendment for fun.*
> *Freedom of religion can be number one.*
> *It's the right to choose our beliefs/religion too.*
> *No one can take what we know to be true."*

Everyone smiles and Dirk sings on:

> *"Freedom of speech/like a day at the beach/*
> *we can share our opinions with a smile and wink/*
> *even go online/tell the world what we think."*

Dirk gets down!

> *"Don't forget freedom of the press.*
> *News and opinions we can express/*
> *through the media/information we share.*
> *When England ruled/you didn't dare.*
> *If you wrote how you felt/the king caused a scare."*

GW nods.

Dirk's on a roll!

> *"With freedom of assembly/we can come together/*
> *rain or shine/no matter the weather.*
> *We can gather to protest/show how we feel.*
> *Once forbidden for you. For us/no big deal."*

GW raises his eyebrows. "It's a right to cherish. A right that's real."

Dirk gives GW a high five, and croons,

"Freedom to petition the government/a cool right too.
We can sign a petition and request something new/
ask to make a change or fix a wrong.
It gives us each a voice that's strong."

GW puffs out his chest, and bellows,

"We Patriots begged England to be heard.
The king wouldn't listen to a single word.
He dismissed our pleas/thought them absurd.
The First Amendment gives you all a voice/
Five big reasons to rejoice."

The StarKids laugh out loud. GW can rap!

Dirk stomps his feet, and sings,

"So, here's to you and the delegate dudes.
We appreciate your efforts and attitudes.
The Constitution protects freedoms and rights.
Gives us the wings to soar to new heights."

GW raises his fists. *"Bravo! Bravo!"*

Zane, Angie, and Piper clap, smiling ear to ear.

"Best song ever!" says Zane.

Angie's laughing when she asks GW,
"How'd the delegates agree on what to put in the
Constitution? We can't even agree on the best
flavor of ice cream."

GW straightens up, shoulders back. "We agreed,
disagreed, and debated for days, but we never
lost sight of our goal to do what was best for our

country. We started with 55 delegates, numbers dwindled, and in the end, 39 of 42 delegates voted in favor of the Constitution."

"I like the way you stay in character when you talk," Zane tells him. "Are all you tour guides actors?"

There's a noise, keys jiggling outside the front door.

GW stands up. *"I am going now,"* he says. *"'Tis well."*

He strides out of the room like an actor strutting off stage.

Angie gets all squinty eyed. "That was weird."

"I know, right!" says Piper. "Isn't he supposed to teach us more stuff?"

A man steps through the front door. He, too, is wearing an old military uniform: an overcoat, waistcoat, and breeches. Another tour guide.

"What are you doing in here?" he asks. "Why are you back there?"

"Chillin' with GW," jokes Angie. "Who are you supposed to be?"

The man glares at her. "No one should be in here."

"We were talking to the other tour guide," Zane tells him.

The man glances around the room. "Other tour guide? How'd you get in this building?"

The StarKids quietly drift to the front of the room. How are they supposed to answer? We tagged a magic flag and popped up in Independence Hall. He'd think they were being cheeky.

"Wait here!" The man turns for the door. "I'm getting security."

"Security?" Dirk whispers. "Time to leave."

The StarKids watch the man charge down the hall and storm out the big wooden door. The hallway has high archways that open to another wood-paneled room that looks like a courtroom. There's a judge's bench, witness stand and two jury boxes. It's symmetrical too. The judge's bench at center has identical windows, doors, and jury boxes on either side.

The StarKids scan the courtroom looking for a way out.

"Let's see if the doors go outside," says Zane.

There's a flash. The magic flag suddenly beams through Dirk's backpack and lights up the courtroom.

"Woohoo!" Angie yells. "We're goin' home."

Dirk takes off his backpack and tries to open the zipper. It's stuck.

"Hurry up!" says Piper. "Chop. Chop."

Dirk keeps pulling on the zipper. It won't budge.

There's a screeching noise. It's the front door.

"They're coming," warns Zane. "What's taking so long?"

"The zipper's broken!" cries Dirk. "I can't—"

Angie grabs the backpack. "We'll rip it open."

Dirk holds the handle, Angie holds a pocket, and they pull in opposite directions.

It's a *tug-of-war!*

Voices echo through the hallway. Footsteps draw closer. Times running out.

Dirk and Angie yank the backpack so hard, the zipper rips wide open and more light pours into the room.

"We did it!" blurts Angie. "Let's get outta here."

"The lights are on in the Supreme Court Room," comes a voice. "They must be in there."

The magic flag flickers, then blinks on and off.

"It's flashing again," says Zane. "Come on!"

Dirk holds out the open backpack. Angie and Zane reach in with two hands and Piper squeezes into the huddle.

"Hurry!" Angie yells. "Tag it!"

Piper can't fit her hands in the backpack, panics, and grabs Angie's arm.

"Not my arm!" Angie screams. "Tag the flag."

CHAPTER
Eleven

WHEN YOU LUCK UPON A STAR.

The suns shining. The creeks gurgling. Piper's <u>clenching</u> Angie's arm. And Angie looks like she just saw a space alien.

"Piper, you made it!" she screams. "And you didn't even tag the flag!"

"I couldn't get my hands in," Piper tells her. "There wasn't room."

Dirk peeks in at the flag in a <u>heap</u> at the bottom of his backpack.

"It flashed again," he says. "What do you think it means?"

"I think it's telling us to tag it," says Zane.

"I don't think we *all* have to tag the flag when it flashes," says Angie. "Piper didn't."

The StarKids go quiet, thinking this over.

"What are you saying?" asks Zane. "That we can tag each other…like a human chain?"

Angie shrugs. "Well, Piper made it and she only tagged me."

Piper finally releases Angie's arm. "We should experiment," she says. "Next time it flashes, Dirk can hold the flag, and we'll tag him."

"It's too <u>risky</u>," says Zane. "What if Dirk goes to the *clue site* and we don't?"

Dirk shrugs, like no big deal. "I'll just ask Ole Magic to bring me home."

Angie reaches behind a bush and scoops up the space helmet. A good thing she left it. She'd never admit it, but wearing the astronaut costume wasn't fun. It's bulky. Hot. And super awkward to move around in.

No more costumes, she thinks.

Dirk picks up a crooked stick and twirls it like a band conductor. He likes to move his hands when his brain is in high gear. And right now, it's in overdrive!

"Let's talk about this later," says Dirk. "We gotta figure out the clue."

Dirk and Zane start along the tree-lined path. Piper stays back to wait for Angie who's twisted around trying to hang the space helmet on her skateboard.

"Do you think the clue is a single word like the first clue?" asks Piper.

"Dunno," Angie says, handing Piper the helmet. "Can you put this on my skateboard?"

Piper drapes the helmet over the skateboard. It looks strange, sort of like a skull on a stick.

"We *flagtagged* to four *clue sites*," says Angie, "and no one has a <u>hunch</u> about the clue. We're not good at this."

"Nope, we're not," Piper agrees.

"This could be impossible."

"Yep, super impossible."

On the trail leading up to the school, the StarKids fall into single file. Zane's at front kicking at the dirt. Dirk's waving the stick. Piper's searching her pockets for a pen. And Angie's straggling behind staring up at the sky and listening to the schoolyard noise.

"If we get the clue," she says, "I hope the stars come out and dance like last time."

"Me too!" says Dirk. "That would be cool!"

"First, we gotta figure it out," says Zane. "Where do we even begin?"

"This calls for a <u>methodical</u> approach," replies Piper. "Let's examine what we saw and heard at each *clue site*...starting with what we saw."

Everyone racks their brain. Amphitheater. Buildings. Steel plant. Factory. Friends House. Trees. Tables. Chairs. People. Pictures. Then, they talk about what they heard.

Nothing out of the ordinary.

Dirk tosses the stick and watches it land on a bush. "This is harder than Ms. Rae's pop quizzes," he says. "And I flunk all those."

Laughter and screams from the schoolyard get louder and louder as they walk up the trail.

"Maybe the clue sites have something in common," says Zane. "But what would a steel mill...guitar factory...Friends House and Independence Hall have in common?"

The StarKids think about this for about 10 seconds, maybe 15. And come up with a big *nothing*.

"Wait!" Piper blurts. "A guitar factory and steel mill have employees who make things."

"The old mill doesn't make steel anymore," says Angie, "and the Quakers don't make things."

Zane picks up a rock and throws it at a tree. "All of them have been in Pennsylvania for a long time," he says, "and people visit them."

The next few minutes are full of guesses and groans, well, mostly groans. Each time one of them guesses the clue, the others groan.

When they reach the crowded schoolyard, it's still free time. Children are everywhere, darting in all directions. Running. Jumping. Climbing. A few counselors are chillin' near the Cub Club, glancing at the kids every so often.

The StarKids drag themselves across the blacktop, <u>scuffing</u> their shoes.

"Mystery-solving is hard work," says Zane. "But we can do it."

Angie notices Billy on the monkey bars <u>hurling</u> bean bags at kids. Smirking. Laughing. Snorting. Lovin' free time!

A teacher calls out, "Billy! Stop it! Please treat others with respect!"

"That's like asking a penguin to fly," jokes Angie.

Billy ignores the teacher, throws another bean bag, hits another kid. Then, he jumps off the monkey bars and scoops up bean bags like a squirrel gathering nuts.

"If Billy had come with us," says Piper. "He would've learned a few things about respect."

"What are you talking about?" asks Angie. "And he's never coming with us."

"I didn't say that." Piper thumbs through her notebook. "At Martin's Guitars, we saw the employees working as a team and treating each other with *respect*."

Dirk picks up a red rubber ball. Zane tries to <u>snatch</u> it out of his hands, but Dirk pulls it away.

"Stop goofing off," Angie tells them. "Piper might be on to something. The man at the steel plant told us that the city preserved the plant to show *respect* for its history."

Piper slows down to read her notes. "At the Friends House, I wrote down that the Quakers *respect* all people and fought for equal rights."

"The Bill of Rights," blurts Dirk. "Our leaders obviously respected our special rights. They adopted the First Amendment to protect them."

"Yeah," Zane agrees. "Good point."

Dirk throws the ball at Zane and it hits him in the leg. It bounces across the blacktop and rolls under the monkey bars. A girl snaps it up, takes a step back and drop kicks it.

Bonk!

It hits Billy in the head.

Dirk and Zane bust up laughing.

"Nice kick," Zane laughs. "Maybe the clue is the word *respect*. Ya gotta *respect* a kick like that."

Boomshakalaka!

Sparkling stars burst into the sky, swirling in and out of each other's arms like square dancers.

Do-Si-Do!

"Look!" exclaims Piper, pointing up at the stars. "The clue is *respect*! R-E-S-P-E-C-T!"

"We did it," Dirk mumbles to himself. "We actually got the clue."

I WISH LUCY COULD SEE THIS.

DIRK. THAT'S NOT THE BIG DIPPER.

Time stops as the StarKids gaze up at the sky in sheer wonder. Heads tilted. Mouths gaped open. Speechless.

Totally freaked out!

Angie breaks the silence. "Remember when Lucy told us to pay attention to what we saw and heard?" she asks. "Well, think about it, we saw examples of *respect* at all the *clue sites*."

"Not Independence Hall!" says Piper. "That was a mess! The guy called security. The zipper got—"

"Hey—we met GW there," says Dirk. "He told us the delegates spent months inside the hall working on the U.S. Constitution."

Piper looks at him. "What's your point?"

Dirk doesn't take his eyes off the dancing stars. "Well…uh…I think it shows they had *respect* for the country and people."

Piper props her hands on her hips. "How?"

"They really cared," he tells her. "They worked hard to help the country…put in tons of time and energy."

"And thought!" adds Zane. "The Constitution was written over 200 years ago and it's still the *supreme law of the land*."

Piper straightens up. Nods politely. "Okay, I get that."

Angie realizes that the schoolyard is still abuzz and glances around. The other kids are running, laughing and hollering. No one seems to notice the spectacle in the sky.

It's play as usual!

"Check it out," she says, pointing to the mob of kids. "I think we're the only ones who can see the stars."

Zane, Piper, and Dirk glance around. Sure enough, no one's looking up at the star-<u>spangled</u> sky.

"What's going on?" mutters Zane. "Doesn't make sense."

As the StarKids glance between the sky and schoolground, a star flashes brightly and slowly floats above the pack. A split second later, the other stars scatter across the sky like seeds in a gust of wind and fade into the sunlight. The lone star drifts toward earth, drawing closer and closer, then suddenly disappears.

Into thin air!

Dirk rips open his backpack and pulls out the magic flag. There's another white star on the <u>canton</u>.

He holds up the flag, smiling. "Whoo-hoo! We got two stars! Only 48 to go!"

The StarKids erupt in laughter and cheers, slapping high fives and bumping fists.

"What a team!" Angie howls. "Together, we can bring 'em all home."

"Nothing seems impossible now," says Piper. "We just gotta put our minds to it."

Zane punches his fists in the air. "Let's go!"

Angie scans the noisy schoolyard and spots Billy under the play structure sitting in the sand.

What's up with him? she wonders. No bean bags. No smirk. No snorts. And he looks sorta frazzled.

Watching him, she gets a strange feeling that Billy saw the stars too.

GLOSSARY

CHAPTER ONE

1. Democracy — government ruled by the people
2. Utter — make a sound with the voice
3. Flail — wave or swing
4. Stumped — confused
5. Fazed — disturbed/bothered
6. Insult — a remark made to hurt someone's feelings
7. Showdown — an argument intended to settle a disagreement
8. Sense — a feeling about something
9. Accomplishment — an achievement
10. Undefeated — has never lost

CHAPTER TWO

1. Tuft — a cluster of strands like hair, grass, or yarn
2. Doomed — likely to fail
3. Fidget — make small movements because you are nervous
4. Slouch — droop or hunch the shoulders
5. Motion — direct someone by moving your head or hands
6. Historic — important in history
7. Document — a written or printed paper that contains information
8. Impressed — someone admires what she/he sees
9. Chomp — chew noisily
10. Uproar — loud noise

CHAPTER THREE

1. Designed — created/ thought up
2. Furrow — make wrinkles or lines
3. Design — a layout of lines and shapes that create a pattern
4. Gleam — shine brightly
5. Gesture — move the head or hands to communicate
6. Majestic — large and beautiful
7. Sophisticated — having wisdom, experience, and knowledge
8. Hearty — energetic, enthusiastic, and cheerful
9. Fumble — handle something clumsily
10. Apologize — say sorry to someone for any hurt you caused

CHAPTER FOUR

1. Hush — a sudden silence
2. Spawn — the eggs of some animals
3. Sprout — grow quickly
4. Rap — a quick hit or knock
5. Stout — thick and strong
6. Leer — look at someone in a nasty, mean way
7. Physical — relates to the body
8. Mental — relates to the mind
9. Snicker — laugh in a mean way
10. Comeback — a quick reply to an insult

DIRK'S NOTES

1. Amend   make a change or add to a law
2. Amendment   a change to a law
3. Express   to talk about or show your feelings, ideas, etc.
4. Press   the media—newspapers, radio, TV, online, etc.
5. Assembly   people gathered together for a specific purpose

CHAPTER FIVE

1. Heebie-jeebies   nervous feelings/ jitters
2. Venture   travel somewhere that could be dangerous
3. Nerve-racking   causes stress and tension
4. Acronym   an abbreviation which consists of the first letter of each word
5. Rebel   disobey rules or fight against authority
6. Aquarium   a tank or glass container where fish live
7. Astronaut   a person who travels into space
8. Billionaire   a person who has one billion dollars or more
9. Stash   hide an object in a secret place
10. Billion   1,000 million

CHAPTER SIX

1. Amphitheater   open area with rows of seats that slope upward
2. Loom   appear in a large and frightening form
3. Vendor   a person or company that sells a product
4. Plant   a factory where a product is manufactured
5. Livelihood   the job a person works to buy the necessities of life (like food and shelter)
6. Refine   make pure/get rid of unwanted material
7. Preserve   keep safe/protect from getting ruined
8. Immigrant   a person who moves from his or her homeland to live in another country permanently.
9. Metaphor   a figure of speech which compares two things that are different from each other, but have something in common.
10. Condiments   something put on food to give it extra flavor

CHAPTER SEVEN

1. Collision — crash/two things colliding
2. Force — a pull or a push
3. Cast — throw out or away
4. Prey — an animal hunted for food
5. Hover — remain in one place in the air
6. Canopy — a layer of something that covers an area
7. Pedestrian — a person who is walking
8. Decked out — be dressed in fancy clothes
9. Technical difficulties — a problem with equipment
10. Grind — rub together

CHAPTER EIGHT

1. Dimly — not bright
2. Swift — move quickly
3. Comical — funny, silly, humorous
4. Activist — a person who works to make political or social change
5. Abolish — put an end to
6. Pant — take quick, short breaths
7. Beckon — move your head or hands to signal someone to come closer
8. Meditate — relax and think deeply
9. Shift — to move from one place to another/change position
10. Sermon — a talk given by a priest, rabbi, or minister on a religious subject

CHAPTER NINE

1. Clamp   fasten something together
2. Precise   exact/accurate
3. Precision   the state of being precise
4. Hightail   move or travel fast
5. Heave   let out a sound (sigh)

CHAPTER TEN

There are no vocabulary words.

CHAPTER ELEVEN

1. Clench   grip, press, or squeeze something
2. Heap   a messy pile
3. Risky   involves risk or danger
4. Hunch   a feeling something is going to happen
5. Methodical follow a method/done in a particular order
6. In common share something (like interests, ideas beliefs, etc.) with another person or thing.
7. Scuff   scrape the feet while walking
8. Hurl   throw something
9. Snatch   quickly grab something
10. Star-spangled studded or spangled with stars
11. Canton   the rectangle on the upper left corner of a flag

PENNSYLVANIA

NICKNAMES: Quaker State / Keystone State
DENONYM: Pennsylvanian
CAPITAL: Harrisburg
MOTTO: Virtue, liberty, and independence
STATE ABBREVIATION: PA
STATE SONG: Pennsylvania
STATE ANIMAL: White-tailed deer
STATE BIRD: Ruffed Grouse
STATE DOG: Great Dane
STATE INSECT: Firefly
STATE FRUIT: Apple
STATE BEVERAGE: Milk

FACTS

Pennsylvania was one of the original 13 colonies, and the second state to join the Union.

In August 1776, the Declaration of Independence was signed in the Independence Hall Assembly Room in Philadelphia, Pennsylvania.

Pennsylvania is landlocked (surrounded by land). All the other American colonies are bordered by the Atlantic Ocean.

FUN FACTS

The first baseball stadium was built in Philadelphia, Pennsylvania.

The chocolate capital of the U.S. is Hershey, Pennsylvania.

The first piano in the U.S. was built in Pennsylvania.

The first public zoo in the U.S. was in Pennsylvania.

Virtue, Liberty, and Independence